ORIGAMI
birds and insects

John Montroll

DOVER PUBLICATIONS, INC.
Mineola, New York

INTRODUCTION

Origami is a challenging and unusual art. It requires square sheets of paper, which are formed into sculptures of animals or other objects by the process of folding.

Origami can be folded from almost any paper, but is most attractive when made from special paper called origami paper. Origami paper is square and usually comes in packets of assorted sizes and colors. It may be found in many variety and hobby stores. Difficult projects are easier to fold if you use the larger sizes of paper. The back side of each sheet of origami paper is white. In this book the colored side of the paper is indicated by the shaded areas.

It is important that you follow the directions carefully. The standard folds, from which the animals are created, are explained in detail at the beginning of the book. I have used the Randlett-Yoshizawa method of notation to indicate the folds.

The following rules should help guide you through the metamorphosis of folding. Examine step one; if there are any creased-folds in the square, fold them first. Make all further folds according to the instructions provided by lines, arrows and captions. Be aware of the instructions in the next step so that you know what each fold will become. Fold slowly and accurately and crease each fold with your fingernail to keep the folds crisp.

Bibliographical Note

This Dover edition, first published in 2004, is a new selections of designs from *Origami for the Enthusiast* (1979) and *Animal Origami for the Enthusiast* (1985) by John Montroll, both previously published by Dover Publications, Inc.

International Standard Book Number: 0-486-43972-0

Manufactured in the United States of America
Dover Publications, Inc., 31 East 2nd Street, Mineola, N.Y. 11501

CONTENTS

Symbols

Lines

‒ ‒ ‒ ‒ ‒ ‒ ‒ ‒ ‒   Valley fold, fold in front.

‒ · ‒ · · ‒ · ‒ · · ‒ ·   Mountain fold, fold behind.

―――――――   Crease line.

·················   X-ray or guide line.

Arrows

Fold in this direction.

Fold behind.

Unfold.

Fold and unfold.

Turn over.

Sink or three dimensional folding.

Place your finger between these layers.

Basic Folds

Rabbit Ear.

To fold a rabbit ear, one corner is folded in half and laid down to a side.

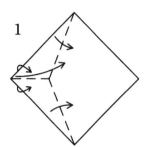

Fold a rabbit ear.

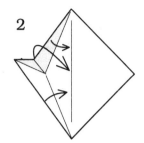

A three-dimensional intermediate step.

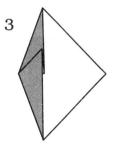

Double Rabbit Ear.

If you were to bend a straw you would be folding the double rabbit ear.

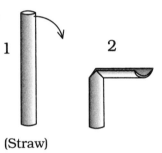

(Straw)

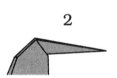

Make a double rabbit ear.

Squash Fold.

In a squash fold, some paper is opened and then made flat. The shaded arrow shows where to place your finger.

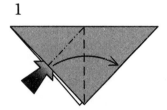

Squash-fold.

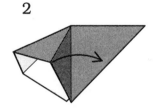

A three-dimensional intermediate step.

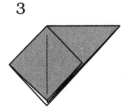

Petal Fold.

In a petal fold, one point is folded up while two opposite sides meet each other.

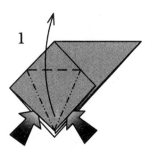

Petal-fold.

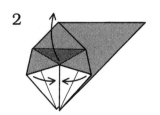

A three-dimensional intermediate step.

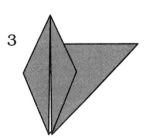

Inside Reverse Fold.

In an inside reverse fold, some paper is folded between layers. Here are two examples.

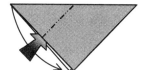 

Reverse-fold.

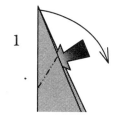 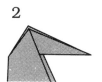

Reverse-fold.

Outside Reverse Fold.

Much of the paper must be unfolded to make an outside reverse fold.

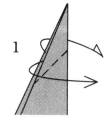 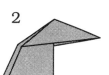

Outside-reverse-fold.

Crimp Fold.

A crimp fold is a combination of two reverse folds.

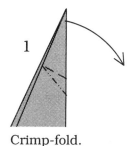 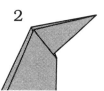

Crimp-fold.

Sink Fold.

In a sink fold, some of the paper without edges is folded inside. To do this fold, much of the model must be unfolded.

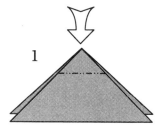 

Sink.

Spread Squash Fold.

A cross between a squash fold and sink fold, some paper in the center is spread apart and then made flat.

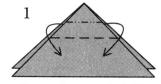 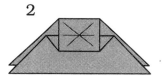

Spread-squash-fold.

Preliminary-fold

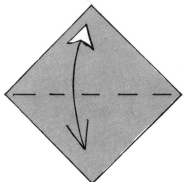

1. Fold diagonally in half, then unfold.

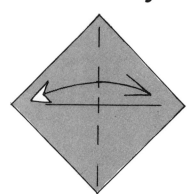

2. Repeat.

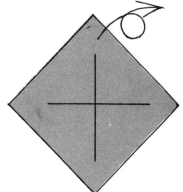

3. Turn over model, then turn clockwise.

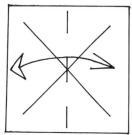

4. Fold in half, then unfold.

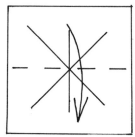

5. Fold in half.

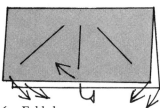

6a. Fold along creases.

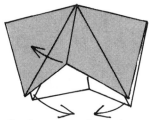

6b. Appearance just before completion.

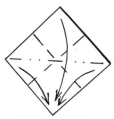

Synopsis of steps 1-6b.

7. **PRELIMINARY-FOLD**

Bird Base

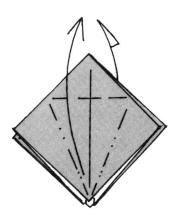

1. Begin with preliminary-fold, then petal-fold both sides.

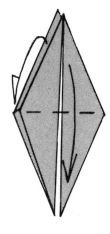

2. Fold tops of both sides down.

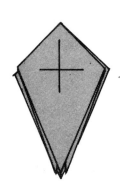

3. **BIRD BASE**

Brontosaurus Base

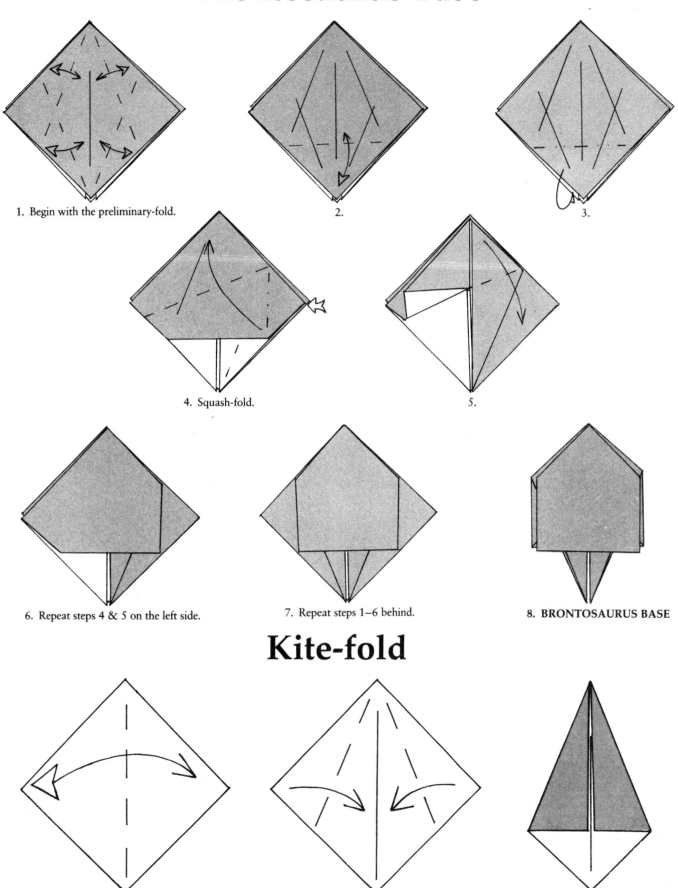

1. Begin with the preliminary-fold.

2.

3.

4. Squash-fold.

5.

6. Repeat steps 4 & 5 on the left side.

7. Repeat steps 1–6 behind.

8. **BRONTOSAURUS BASE**

Kite-fold

1. Fold diagonally in half, then unfold.

2. Valley-fold along lines to center crease.

3. **KITE-FOLD**

Water Bomb Base

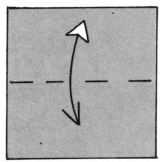

1. Fold horizontally in half, then unfold.

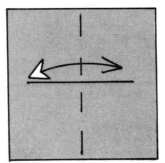

2. Fold vertically in half, then unfold.

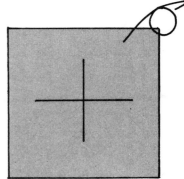

3. Turn model over.

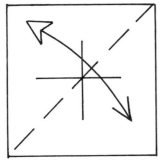

4. Fold diagonally in half, then unfold.

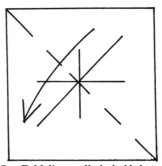

5. Fold diagonally in half along dashed line.

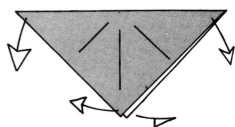

6. Fold along creases (Model will open slightly.)

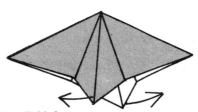

7. Fold along creases.

8. **WATER BOMB BASE**

Blintz-fold

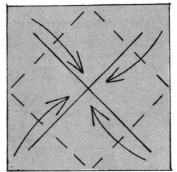

1. Fold and unfold diagonally in half to form creases as shown, then fold four corners to center.

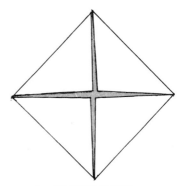

2. **BLINTZ-FOLD**

Pleat-fold

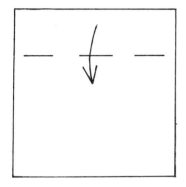

1. Valley-fold. Fold forward.

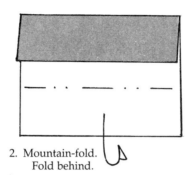

2. Mountain-fold.
   Fold behind.

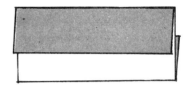

3. Finished model displaying both
   folds.

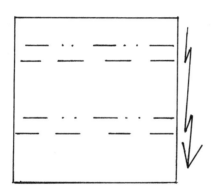

4. Combination of mountain-and
   valley-folds.

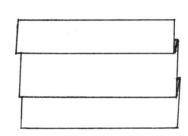

5. **PLEAT-FOLD**

Vulture

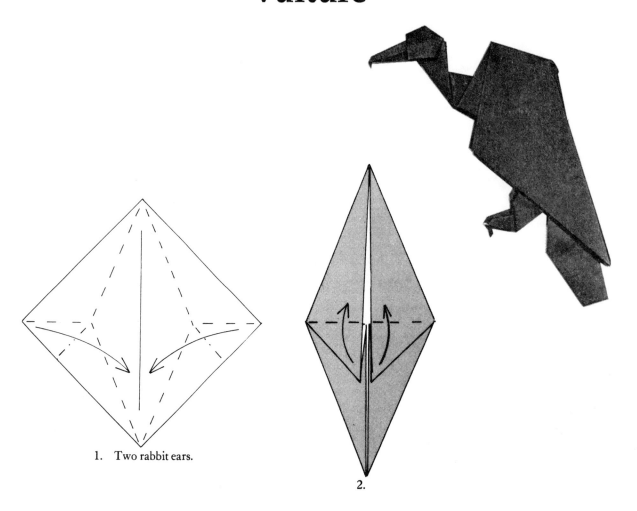

1. Two rabbit ears.

2.

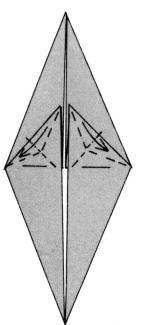

3. Two rabbit ears.

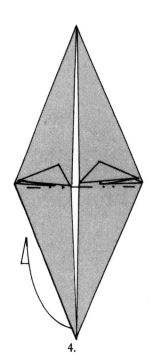

4.

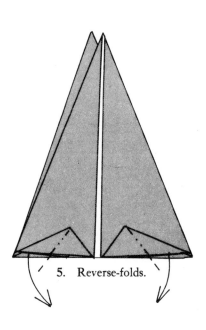

5. Reverse-folds.

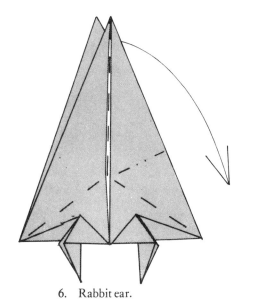

6. Rabbit ear.

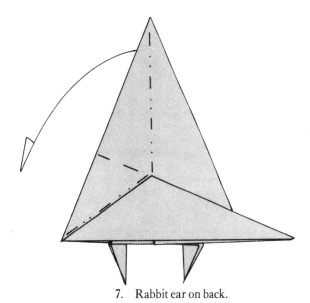

7. Rabbit ear on back.

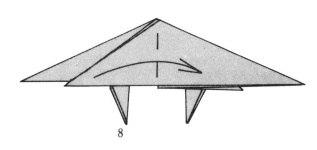

8

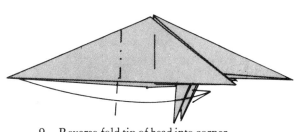

9. Reverse-fold tip of head into corner of top wing.

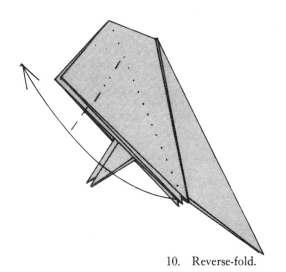

10. Reverse-fold.

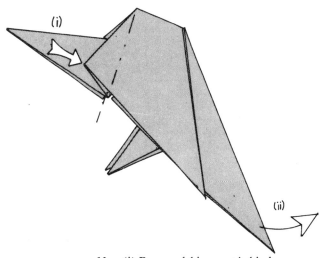

11. (i) Reverse-fold; repeat behind.
    (ii) Slide tail out.

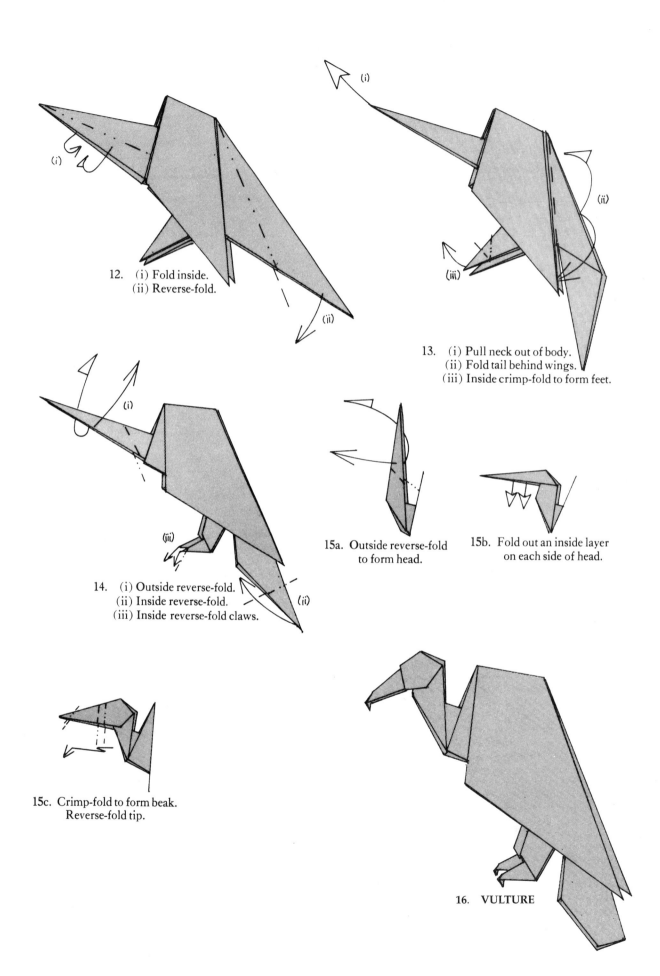

12. (i) Fold inside.
(ii) Reverse-fold.

13. (i) Pull neck out of body.
(ii) Fold tail behind wings.
(iii) Inside crimp-fold to form feet.

14. (i) Outside reverse-fold.
(ii) Inside reverse-fold.
(iii) Inside reverse-fold claws.

15a. Outside reverse-fold to form head.

15b. Fold out an inside layer on each side of head.

15c. Crimp-fold to form beak. Reverse-fold tip.

16. **VULTURE**

Ostrich

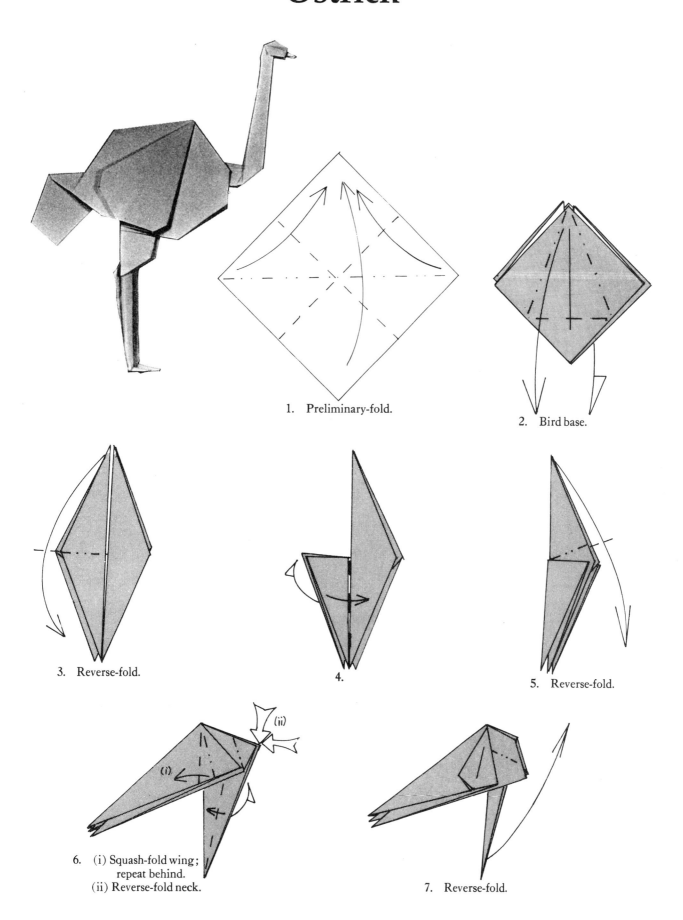

1. Preliminary-fold.

2. Bird base.

3. Reverse-fold.

4.

5. Reverse-fold.

6. (i) Squash-fold wing; repeat behind.
   (ii) Reverse-fold neck.

7. Reverse-fold.

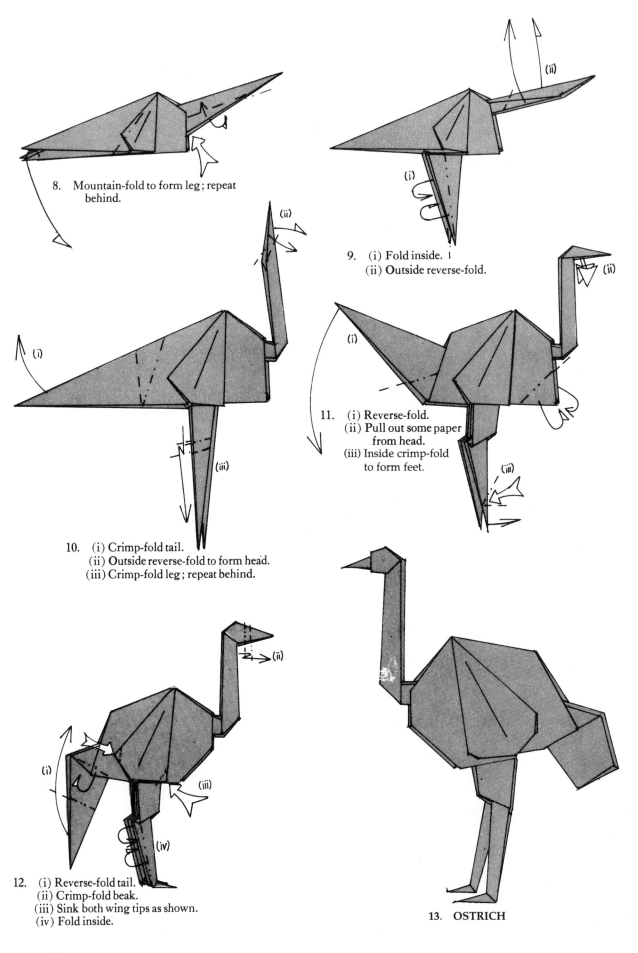

8. Mountain-fold to form leg; repeat
    behind.

9. (i) Fold inside.
    (ii) Outside reverse-fold.

10. (i) Crimp-fold tail.
    (ii) Outside reverse-fold to form head.
    (iii) Crimp-fold leg; repeat behind.

11. (i) Reverse-fold.
    (ii) Pull out some paper
         from head.
    (iii) Inside crimp-fold
          to form feet.

12. (i) Reverse-fold tail.
    (ii) Crimp-fold beak.
    (iii) Sink both wing tips as shown.
    (iv) Fold inside.

13. **OSTRICH**

Stork

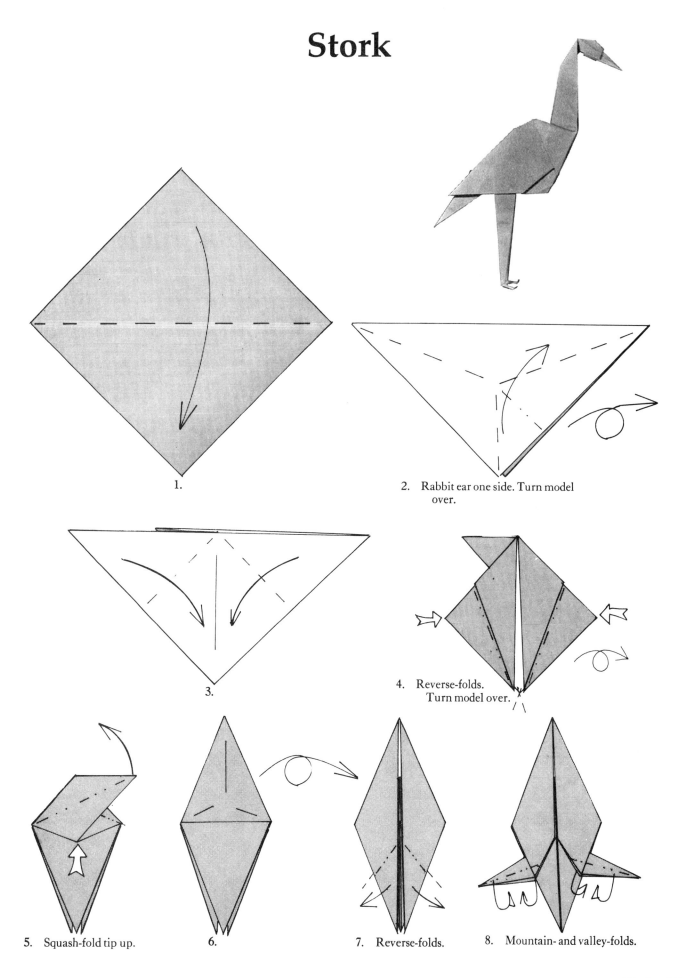

1.

2. Rabbit ear one side. Turn model over.

3.

4. Reverse-folds. Turn model over.

5. Squash-fold tip up.

6.

7. Reverse-folds.

8. Mountain- and valley-folds.

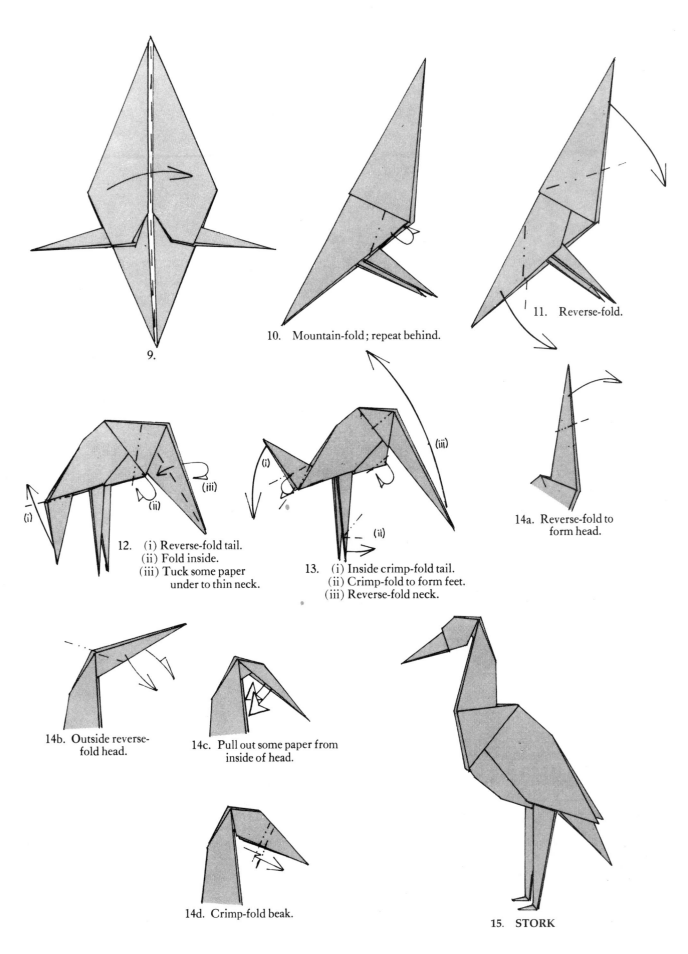

9.

10. Mountain-fold; repeat behind.

11. Reverse-fold.

12. (i) Reverse-fold tail.
    (ii) Fold inside.
    (iii) Tuck some paper under to thin neck.

13. (i) Inside crimp-fold tail.
    (ii) Crimp-fold to form feet.
    (iii) Reverse-fold neck.

14a. Reverse-fold to form head.

14b. Outside reverse-fold head.

14c. Pull out some paper from inside of head.

14d. Crimp-fold beak.

15. STORK

Robin

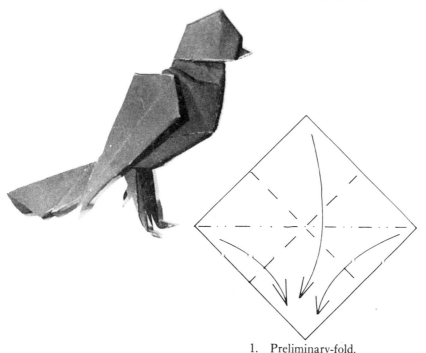

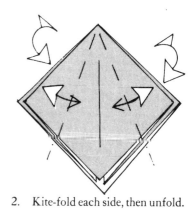

1. Preliminary-fold.

2. Kite-fold each side, then unfold.

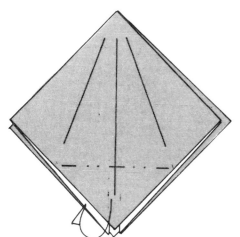

3. Fold top layer behind.

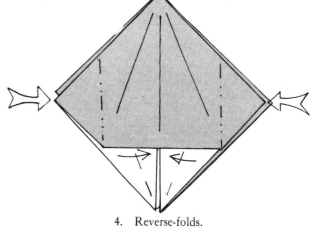

4. Reverse-folds.

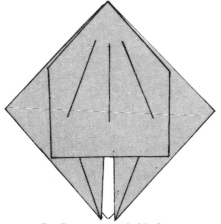

5. Repeat step 4 behind.

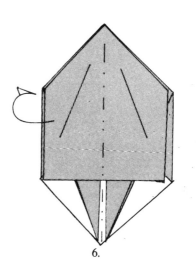

6.

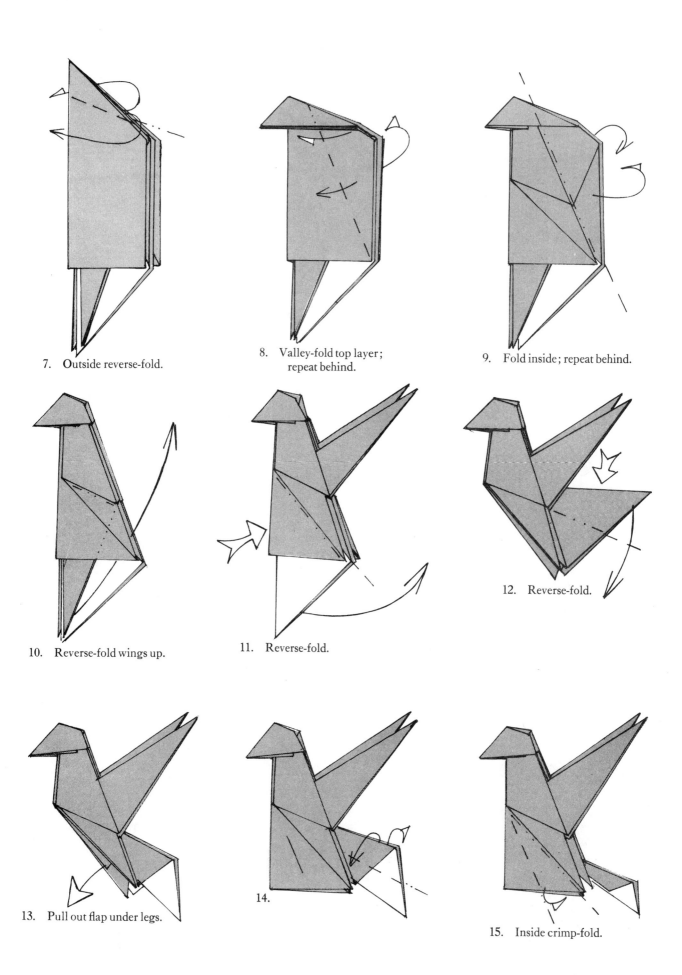

7. Outside reverse-fold.

8. Valley-fold top layer; repeat behind.

9. Fold inside; repeat behind.

10. Reverse-fold wings up.

11. Reverse-fold.

12. Reverse-fold.

13. Pull out flap under legs.

14.

15. Inside crimp-fold.

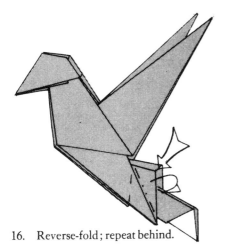

16.   Reverse-fold; repeat behind.

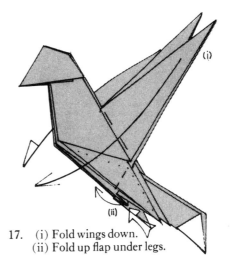

17.   (i) Fold wings down.
      (ii) Fold up flap under legs.

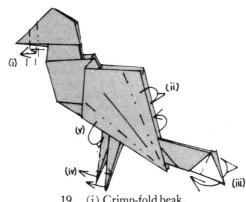

18.   (i) Inside crimp-fold neck.
      (ii) Squash-fold wings.
      (iii) Double rabbit ear the legs.

19.   (i) Crimp-fold beak.
      (ii) Fold inside.
      (iii) Outside reverse-fold tail.
      (iv) Crimp-fold feet.
      (v) Fold inside.

20.   ROBIN

Crane

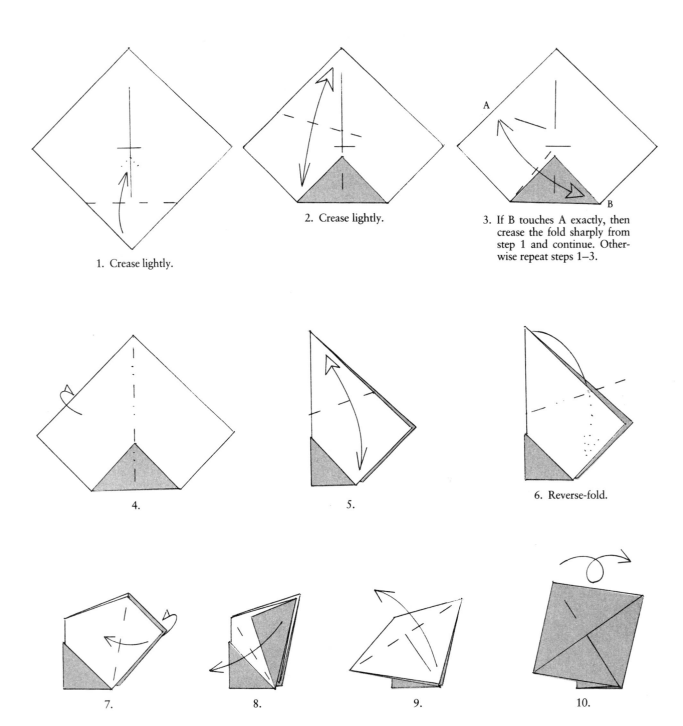

1. Crease lightly.

2. Crease lightly.

3. If B touches A exactly, then crease the fold sharply from step 1 and continue. Otherwise repeat steps 1–3.

4.

5.

6. Reverse-fold.

7.

8.

9.

10.

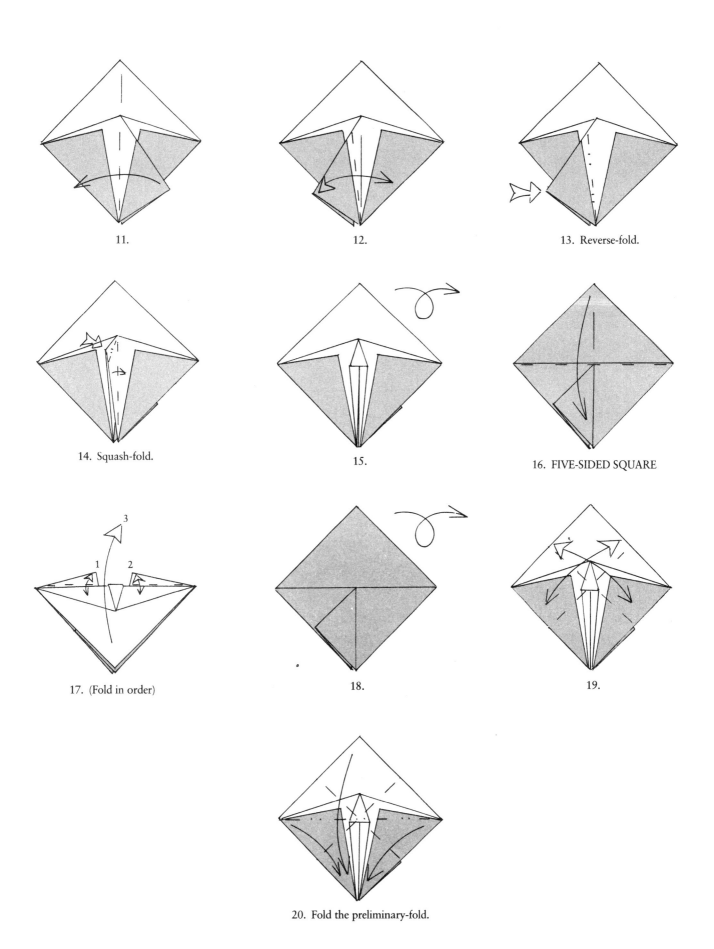

11.

12.

13. Reverse-fold.

14. Squash-fold.

15.

16. FIVE-SIDED SQUARE

17. (Fold in order)

18.

19.

20. Fold the preliminary-fold.

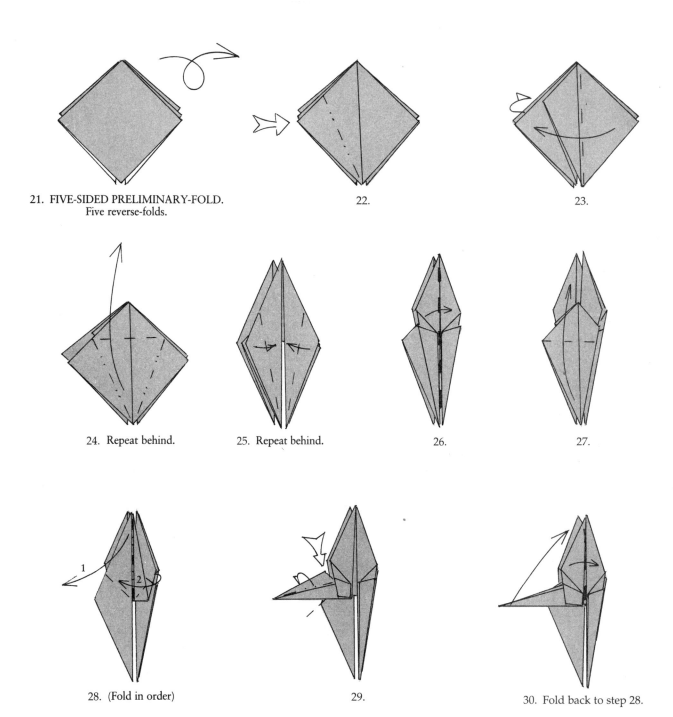

21. FIVE-SIDED PRELIMINARY-FOLD.
Five reverse-folds.

22.

23.

24. Repeat behind.

25. Repeat behind.

26.

27.

28. (Fold in order)

29.

30. Fold back to step 28.

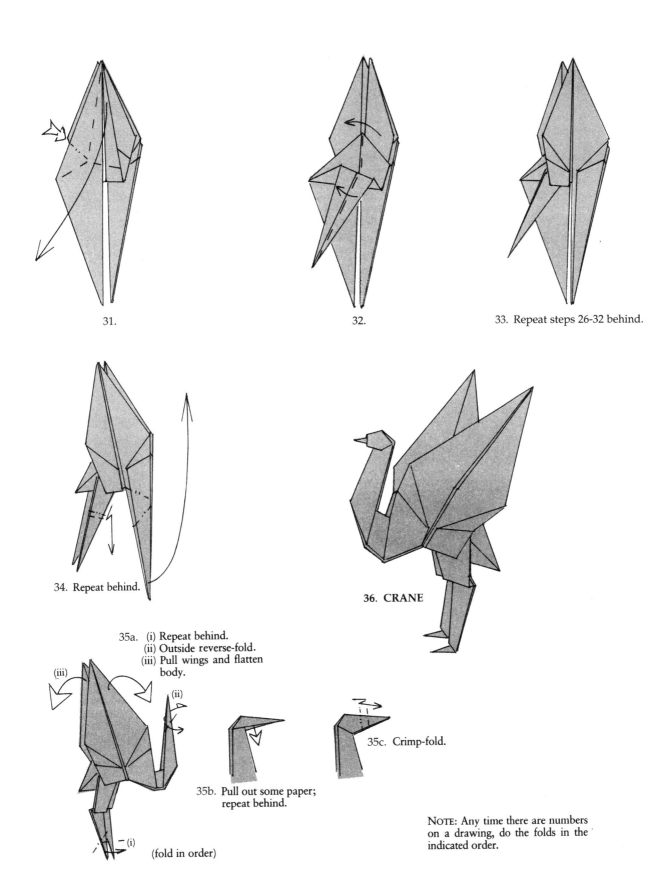

31.

32.

33. Repeat steps 26-32 behind.

34. Repeat behind.

35a. (i) Repeat behind.
  (ii) Outside reverse-fold.
  (iii) Pull wings and flatten body.

(iii)

(ii)

(i)

(fold in order)

35b. Pull out some paper; repeat behind.

35c. Crimp-fold.

36. CRANE

NOTE: Any time there are numbers on a drawing, do the folds in the indicated order.

Swan

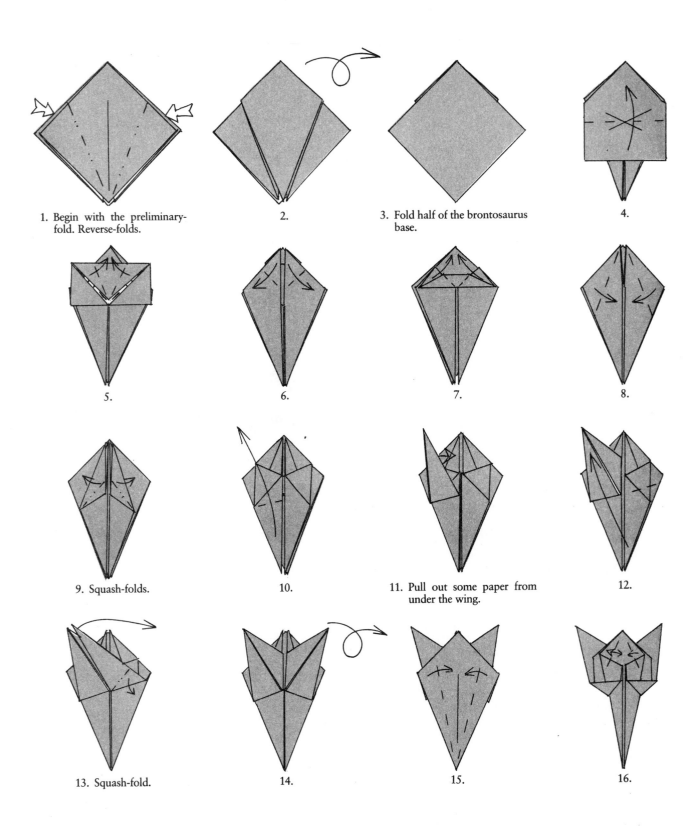

1. Begin with the preliminary-fold. Reverse-folds.

2.

3. Fold half of the brontosaurus base.

4.

5.

6.

7.

8.

9. Squash-folds.

10.

11. Pull out some paper from under the wing.

12.

13. Squash-fold.

14.

15.

16.

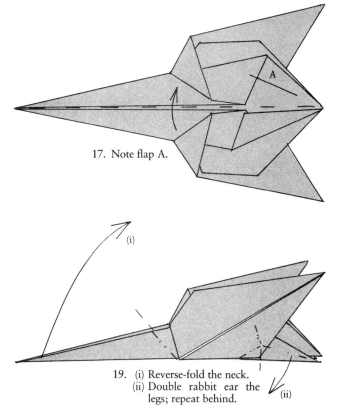

17. Note flap A.

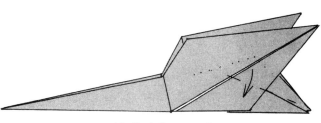

18. Tuck flap A inside.

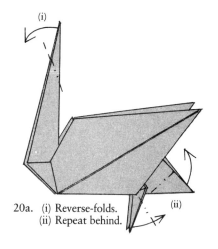

19. (i) Reverse-fold the neck.
(ii) Double rabbit ear the legs; repeat behind.

20a. (i) Reverse-folds.
(ii) Repeat behind.

20b. Outside reverse-fold.

20c. Pull out some paper from inside; repeat behind.

20d.

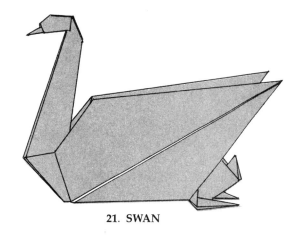

21. SWAN

Owl

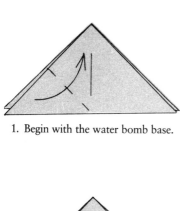

1. Begin with the water bomb base.

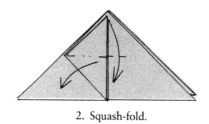

2. Squash-fold.

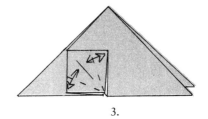

3.

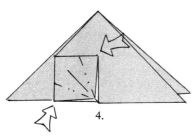

4.

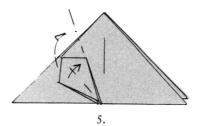

5.

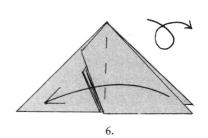

6.

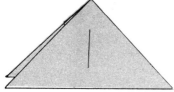

7. Fold steps 1–5 on the right side.

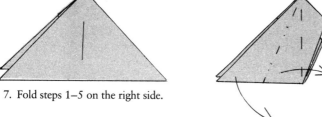

8. Squash fold; repeat behind.

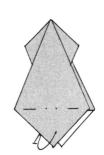

9. Repeat behind.

10.

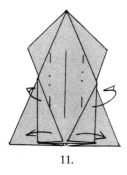

11.

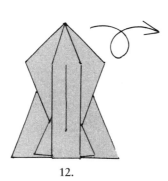

12.

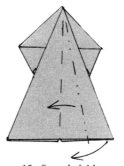

13. Squash-fold.

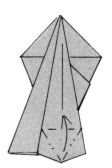

14. Petal-fold.

15.

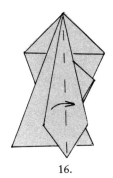

16.

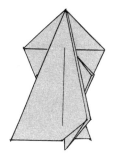

17. Repeat steps 13–16 on the
left side.

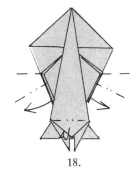

18.

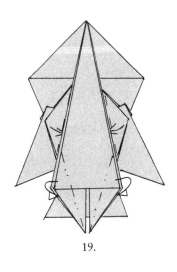

19.

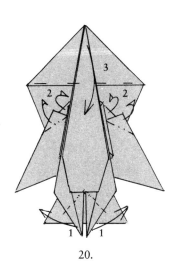

20.

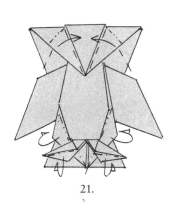

21.

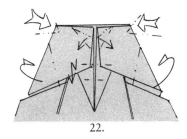

22.

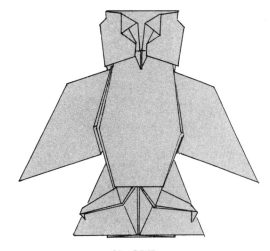

23. OWL

Moth

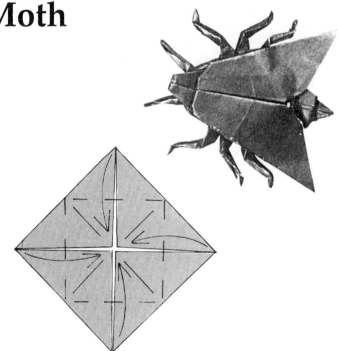

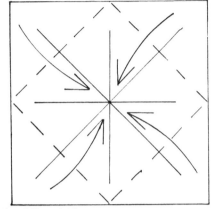

1. Blintz-fold.

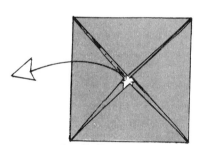

3. Pull out one corner.

2. Blintz-fold again.

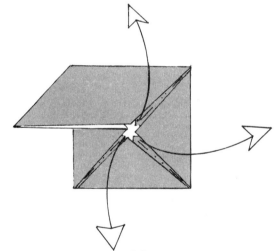

4. Pull out remaining corners.

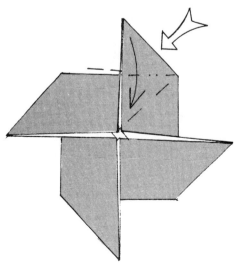

5. Squash-fold.

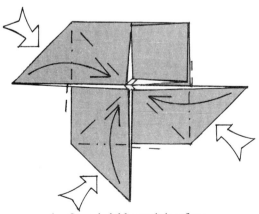

6. Squash-fold remaining flaps.

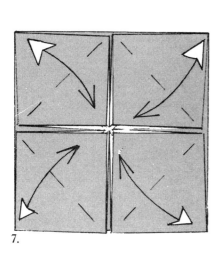

7.

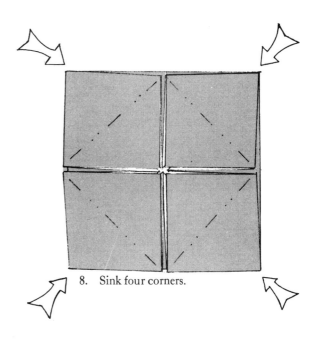

8. Sink four corners.

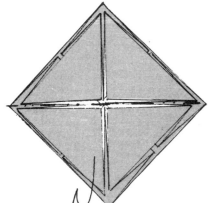

9. Mountain-fold model in half.

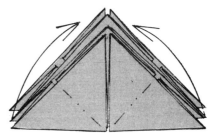

10. Reverse-fold middle flaps.

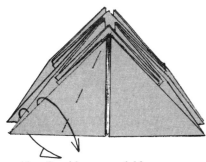

11. Outside reverse-fold.

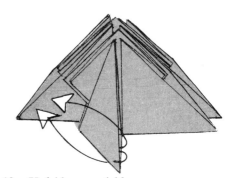

12. Unfold reverse-fold.

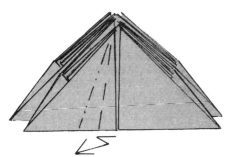

13. Outside crimp-fold.

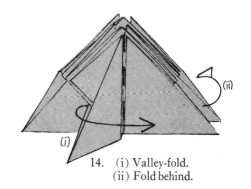

14. (i) Valley-fold.
    (ii) Fold behind.

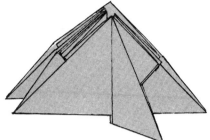

15. Repeat steps 11–13 on left side.

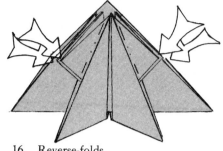

16. Reverse-folds.

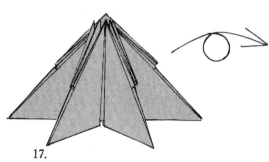

17.

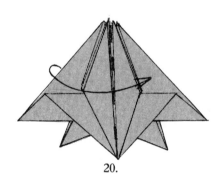

18. Petal-fold inside, while folding outer flap down.

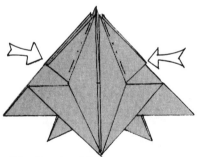

19. Reverse-folds.

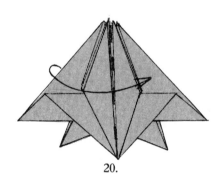

20.

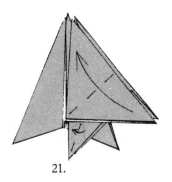

21.

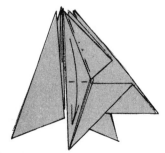

22. Petal-fold.

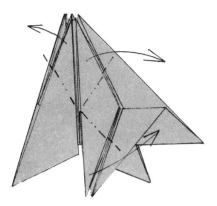

23. Reverse-fold 3 legs as shown.

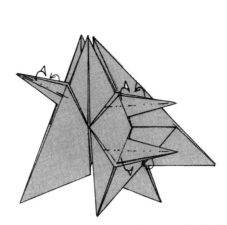

24. Mountain-fold inside; repeat behind.

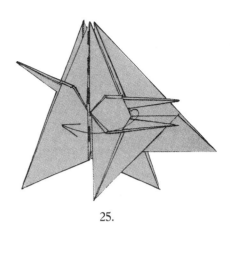

25.

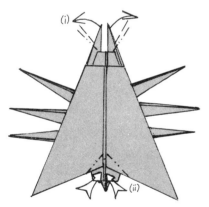

26. Repeat steps 20–25 on right side.

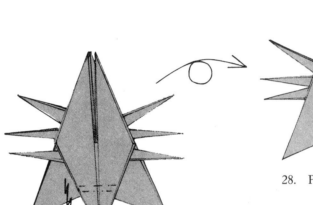

27. Pleat-fold tail. Turn model over.

28. Pleat-fold to form head.

29. (i) Reverse-folds.
    (ii) Sink.

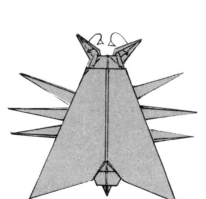

30. Reverse-folds; repeat behind.

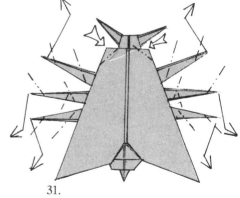

31.

32. **MOTH**

Stink Bug

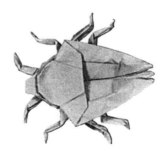

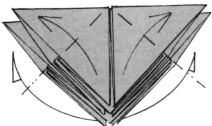

1. Begin with step 11 of Moth turned clockwise. Valley-fold; repeat behind.

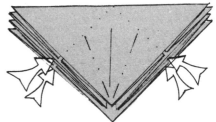

2. Reverse-fold lower 4 flaps.

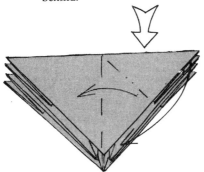

3. Squash-fold.

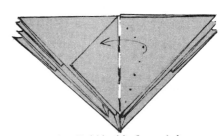

4. Fold inside flap to left.

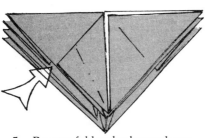

5. Reverse-fold so that bottom layer covers inside flap in step 4.

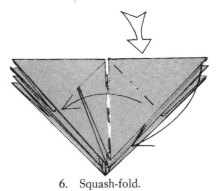

6. Squash-fold.

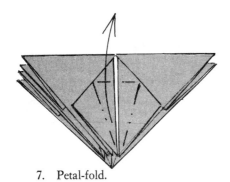

7. Petal-fold.

8.

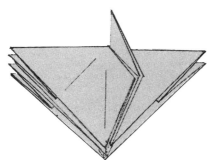

9. Repeat steps 3–8 on left side.

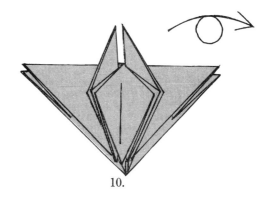

10.

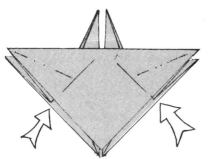

11. Reverse-folds.

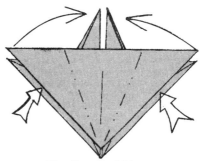

12. Reverse-folds.

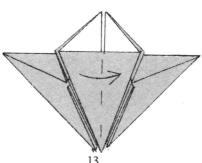

13.

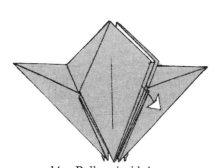

14. Pull out inside layer.

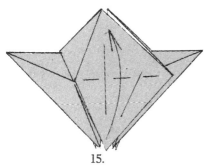

15.

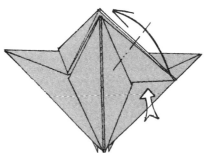

16. Reverse-fold.

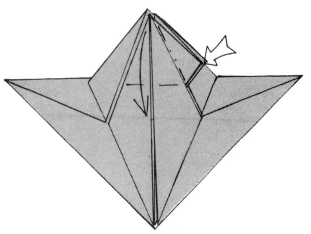

17. Petal-fold.

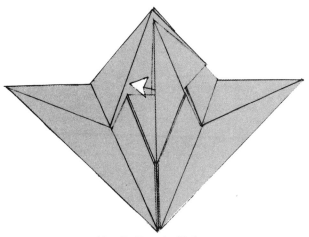

18. Pull out inside layers.

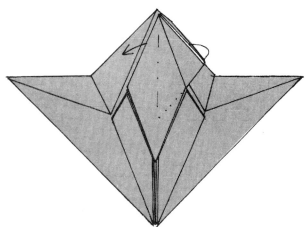

19. Reverse-fold inside layer.

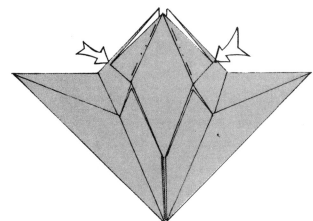

20. Reverse-folds.

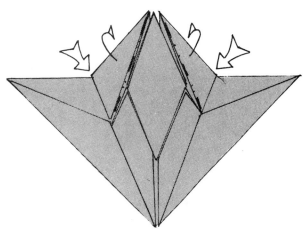

21. Reverse-folds.

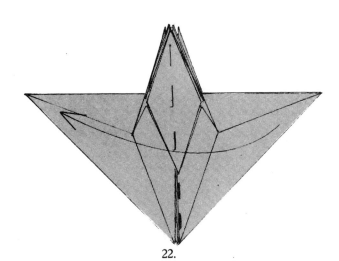

22.

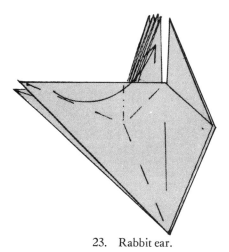

23. Rabbit ear.

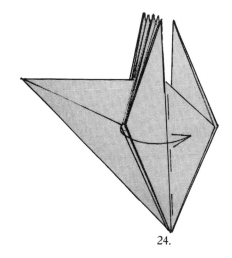

24.

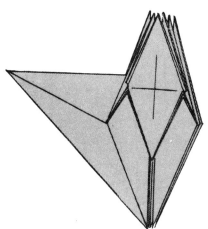

25. Repeat steps 22–24 on left side.

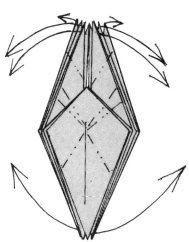

27. Reverse-fold to form legs and antennae.

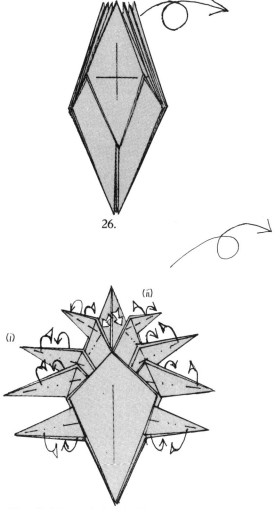

26.

28. (i) Mountain fold inside; repeat behind.
    (ii) Reverse-fold antennae.

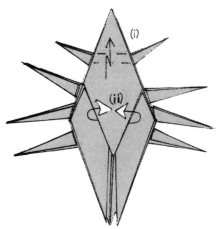

29. (i) Pleat-fold.
    (ii) Pull wings out and fold on top.

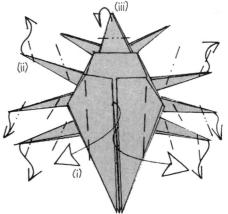

30. (i) Fold wings out.
    (ii) Reverse-fold each leg twice.
    (iii) Mountain-fold.

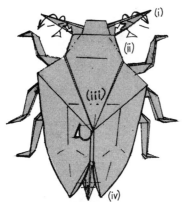

31. (i) Outside reverse-fold.
    (ii) Reverse-fold.
    (iii) Tuck under.
    (iv) Pleat-fold tail.

32. **STINK BUG**

Beetle

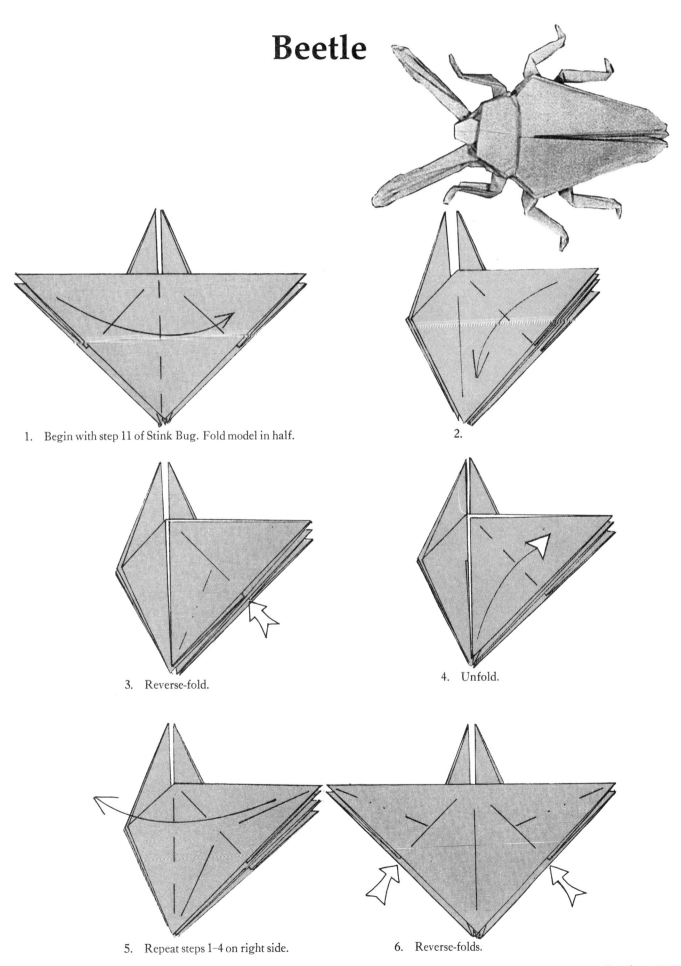

1. Begin with step 11 of Stink Bug. Fold model in half.

2.

3. Reverse-fold.

4. Unfold.

5. Repeat steps 1–4 on right side.

6. Reverse-folds.

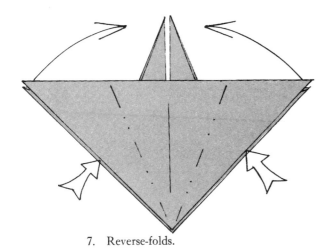

7. Reverse-folds.

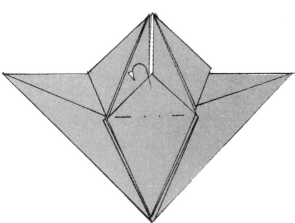

8. Reverse-folds.

9. Mountain-fold flap.

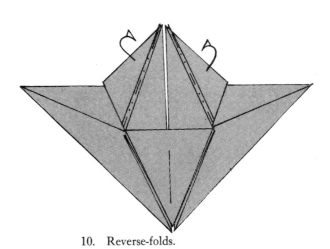

10. Reverse-folds.

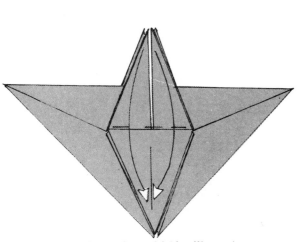

11. Fold flap down. (Several folds will open.)

12.

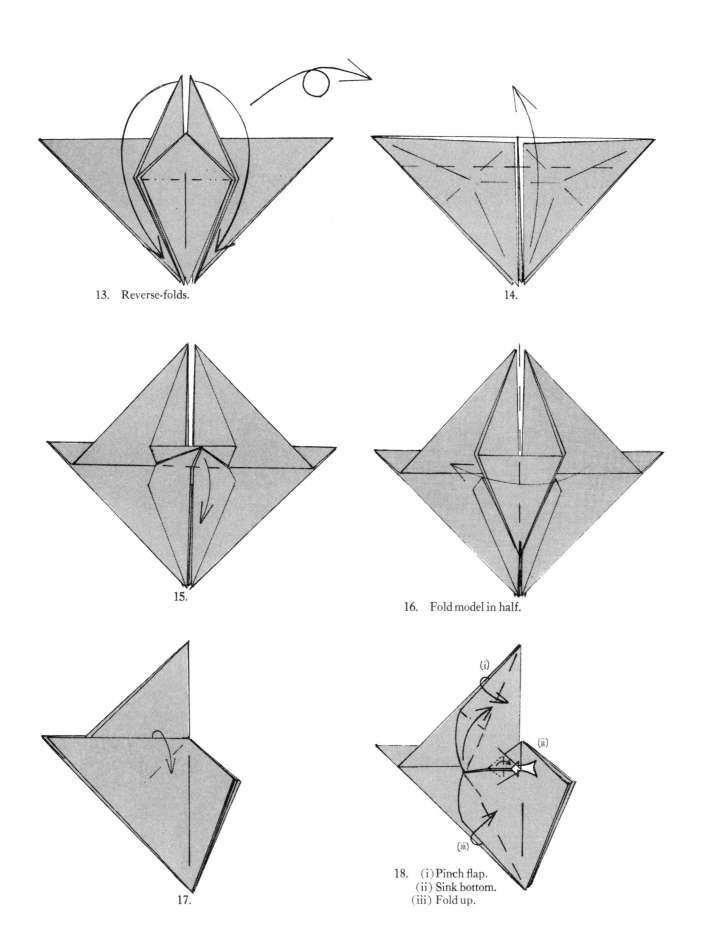

13. Reverse-folds.

14.

15.

16. Fold model in half.

17.

18. (i) Pinch flap.
    (ii) Sink bottom.
   (iii) Fold up.

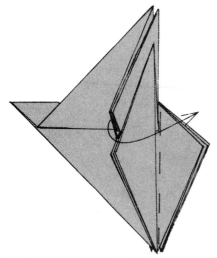

19. Repeat steps 16–19 on left side.

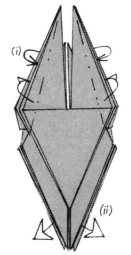

20. (i) Fold inside; repeat behind.
    (ii) Slide out part of wing.

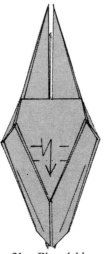

21a. Pleat-fold.

21b. Squash-folds.

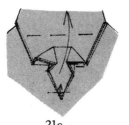

21c.

21d. Reverse-folds.

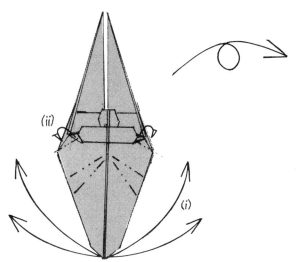

22. (i) Reverse-fold to form legs.
     (ii) Tuck inside. Turn model over.

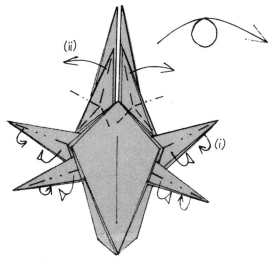

23. (i) Mountain-fold inside; repeat behind
         on remaining back legs.
     (ii) Rabbit ear. Turn model over.

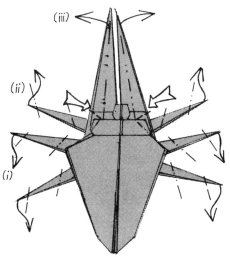

24. (i) Inside reverse-fold each back leg twice.
     (ii) Outside reverse-fold each front leg twice.
     (iii) Double rabbit ear antennae.

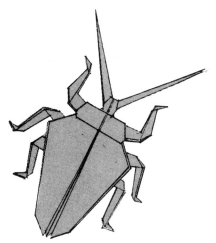

25. BEETLE

Grasshopper

1. . Blintz-fold.

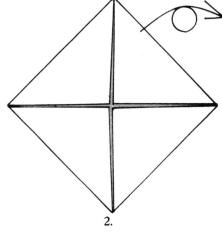

2.

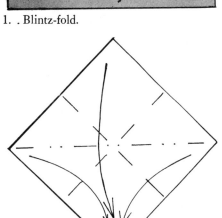

3.   Preliminary-fold.

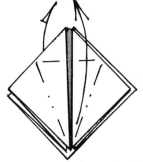

4.   Petal-fold front and back.

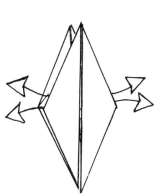

5.   Pull out inner layers.

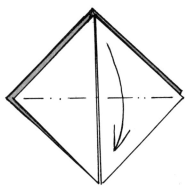

6.   Valley-fold front layer.

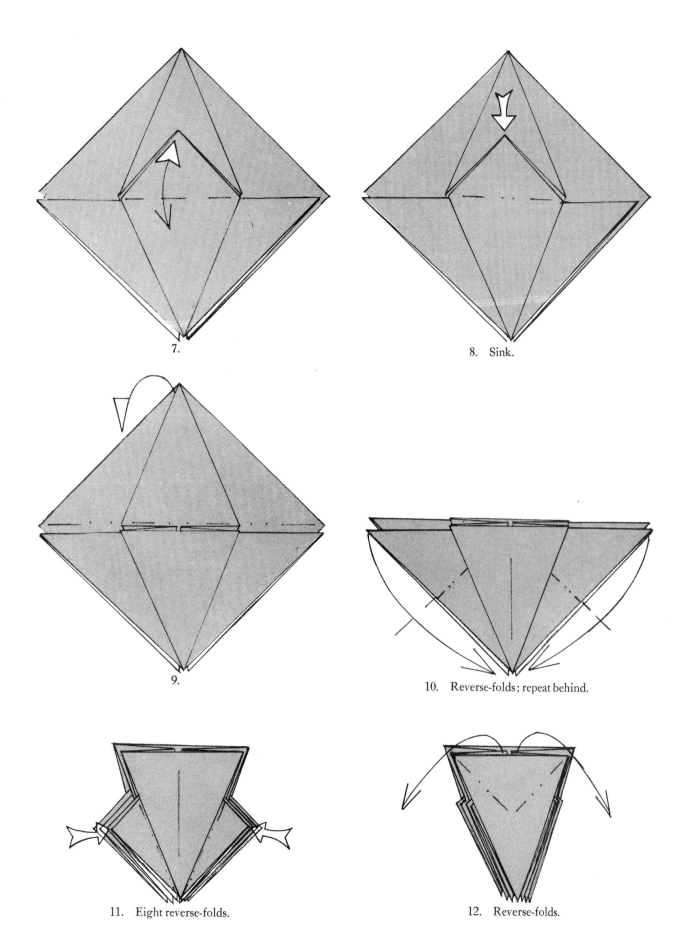

7.

8. Sink.

9.

10. Reverse-folds; repeat behind.

11. Eight reverse-folds.

12. Reverse-folds.

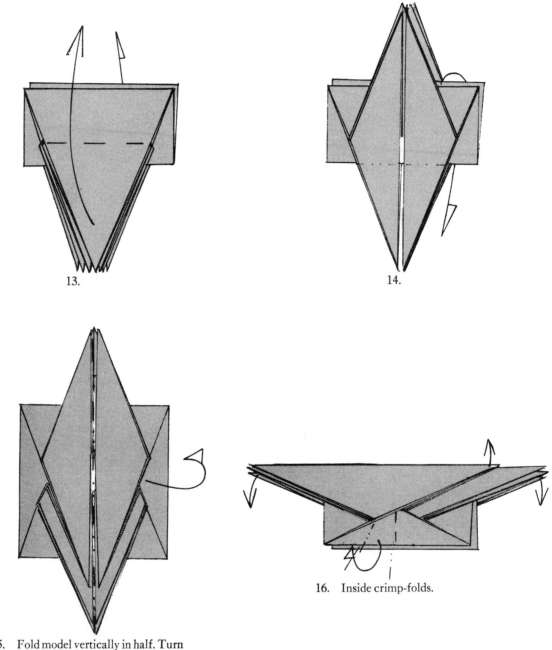

13.

14.

15. Fold model vertically in half. Turn
     counterclockwise.

16. Inside crimp-folds.

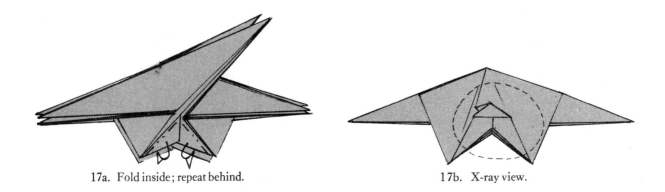

17a. Fold inside; repeat behind.

17b. X-ray view.

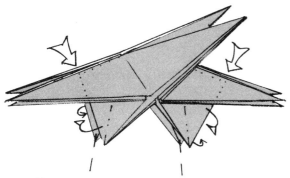

18. Reverse-folds; repeat behind.

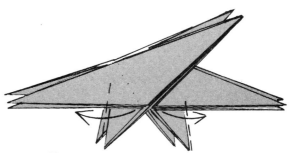

19. Valley-fold top layer; repeat behind.

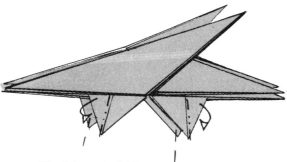

20. Mountain-fold; repeat behind.

21. Reverse-fold lowest layer of top flaps; repeat behind.

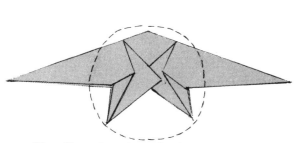

21a. X-ray view of completed reverse-folds.

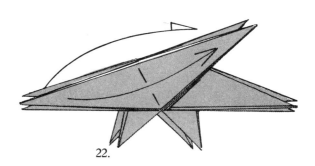

22.

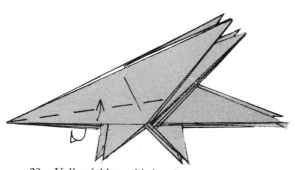

23. Valley-fold one third as shown.

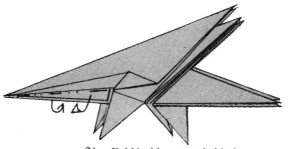

24. Fold inside; repeat behind.

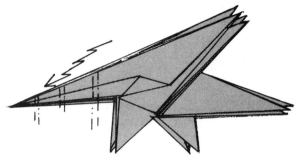

25. Crimp-fold tail.

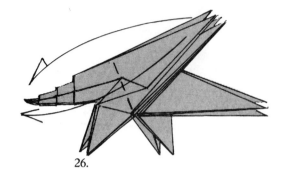

26.

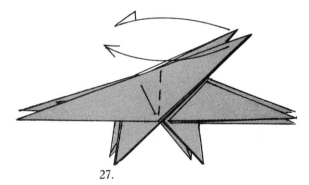

27.

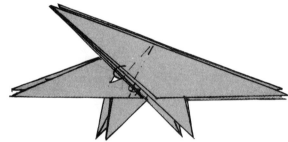
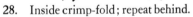

28. Inside crimp-fold; repeat behind.

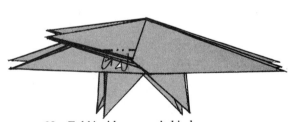

29. Fold inside; repeat behind.

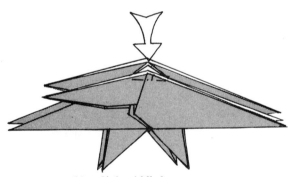

30. Sink middle layer.

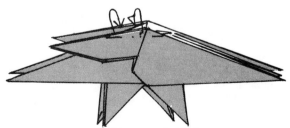

31. Fold inside; repeat behind.

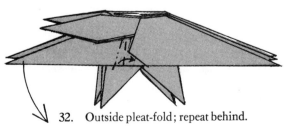

32. Outside pleat-fold; repeat behind.

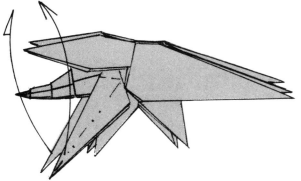

33. Petal-fold; repeat behind.

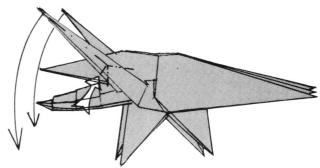

34. Double rabbit ear legs.

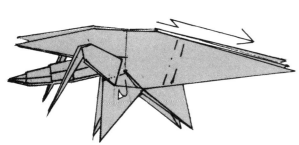

35. Pleat-fold; repeat behind.

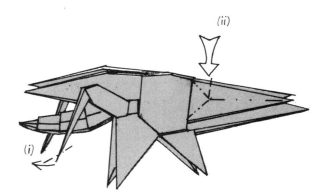

36. (i) Reverse-fold; repeat behind.
    (ii) Double rabbit ear; repeat behind.

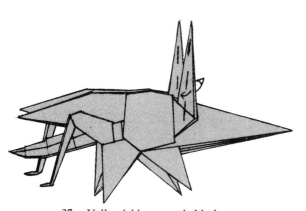

37. Valley-folds; repeat behind.

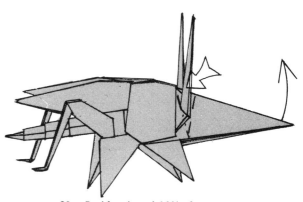

38. Inside crimp-fold head.

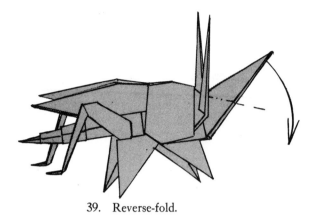

39. Reverse-fold.

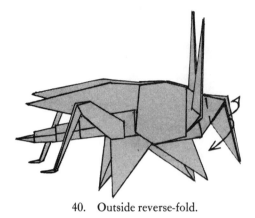

40. Outside reverse-fold.

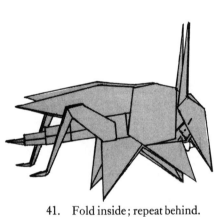
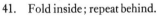

41. Fold inside; repeat behind.

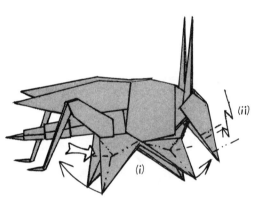

42. (i) Double rabbit ear legs; repeat behind.
   (ii) Crimp-fold mouth.

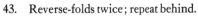

43. Reverse-folds twice; repeat behind.

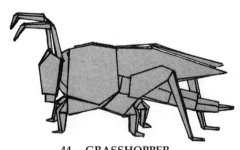

44. **GRASSHOPPER**